UFOs

Is there life out there?

Author: **Rosy Border**
Series Editor: **John Foster**

COLLINS
Sound*bites*

Published by HarperCollins *Publishers* Limited
77-85 Fulham Palace Road
Hammersmith
London
W6 8JB

.www.**Collins**Education.com
On-line support for schools and colleges

© Rosy Border 2000
First published 2000

ISBN Level 1: 0-00-323083-X

British Library Cataloguing in Publication Data
A catalogue record for this publication is available from the
British Library

Dedication
For John who kept the coffee coming

Acknowledgements
The following permissions to reproduce material are gratefully acknowledged:

Science Photo Library, p4 (Julian Baum), p8 (Frank Zullo), p16 (David
Hardy), p27 (David Parker), p38 (Mehau Kulyk), p40 (John Sandford), p42
(David Parker); Fortean Picture Library, p6 (Woody Akins), p7 (Andy
Radford), p12 (Gary Marshall), p14 (Paul Villa), p18; Frank Spooner Pictures
pp29, 36; Science Museum/Science and Society Picture Library, p41; Oxford
Scientific Films (Satoshi Kuribayashi, firefly, p42; Starland Picture Library,
p43 (ESA), p46 (Seth Shostak), p47 (NASA).

Illustrated by Paul McCaffrey

Cover design and internal design by Ken Vail Graphic Design, Cambridge

Cover photograph by Victor Habbick Visions/Science Photo Library

Commissioning Editor: Helen Clark

Edited by Lucy Hobbs

Production: Sarah Bacon

Printed and bound by Printing Express, Hong Kong

You might also like to visit
www.fireandwater.co.uk
The book lover's website

Contents

Is there life out there?

Lots of people say they have seen a UFO.
This is what one man said.

'It was a very large object which had two lights.
It flew away very fast.'

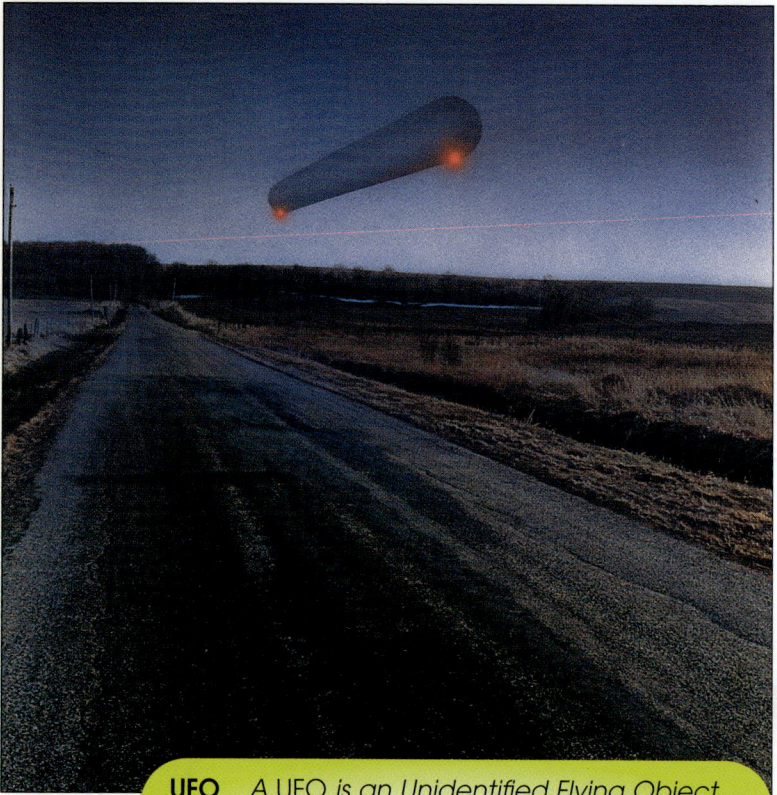

UFO A UFO is an Unidentified Flying Object.
It is something that has been seen flying
in the sky, but no one can say what it is.

Some people think there is life in space.

Other people are not sure.

What is a UFO?

One man who saw a UFO took a picture of it.
Some people think it was a shooting star.

Is this a shooting star or a UFO?

shooting star   *A piece of rock or metal that burns brightly when it comes close to the Earth*

Every year more people say they see UFOs.
We cannot always tell what they really are.

A UFO is an Unidentified Flying Object.

Where do UFOs come from?

Do UFOs come from other worlds?
A lot of people think they do.
Are they right?

Is there life out there?

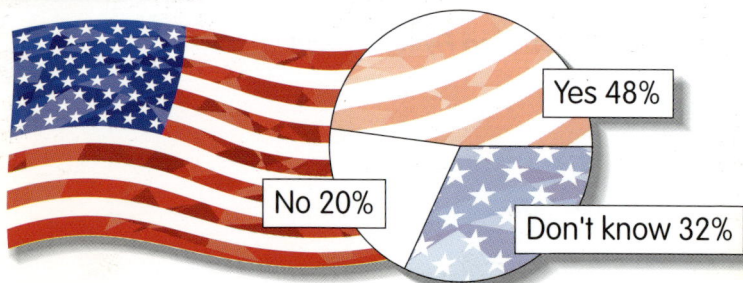

Yes 48%

No 20%

Don't know 32%

What people in the USA think

satellite   *An object sent into space which goes round the Earth.*

The first UFOs

People have been seeing UFOs for a long time.

Egypt, 1500 BC

The King and his men saw 'rings of fire, brighter than the sun'.

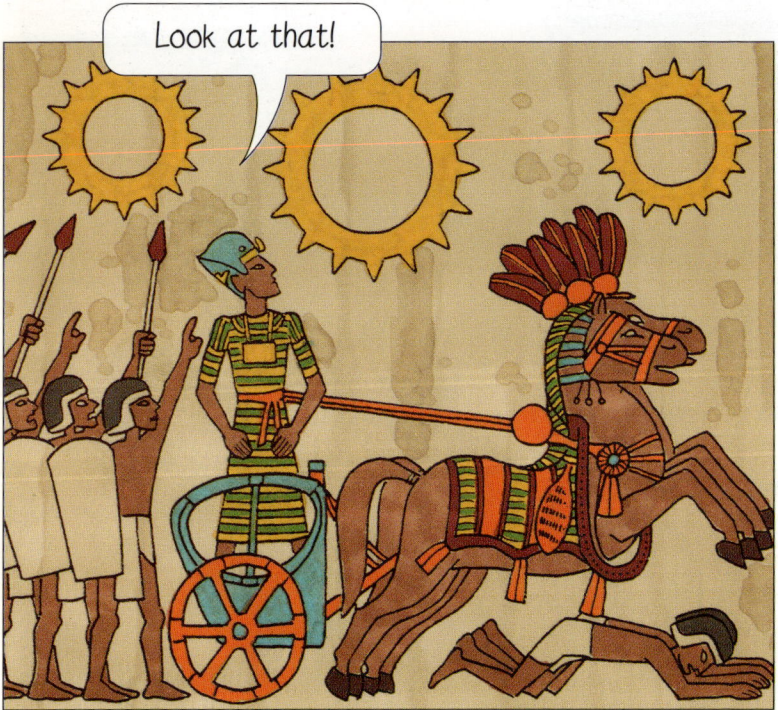

Look at that!

BC BC stands for 'Before Christ'. It is used to measure time before the Year 0.

Italy, 90 BC

Some people said they saw a ball of fire.

'It fell from the sky. Then it went up again. It was going round like a wheel.'

What is that?

The first 'Flying saucers'

USA – 24 June 1947

A plane was flying over some hills.

The pilot saw nine silver objects in the sky.

They were flying very fast.

flying saucer *A flying object shaped like a saucer (a small round dish on which a cup is put)*

They were big and round.

'They looked like plates,' he told a newspaper reporter.

'Flying saucers!' said the reporter.

We still use the name today.

They looked like plates.

UFO Crash!

Roswell, USA – July 1947

Soon lots of people were seeing flying saucers.

One man found bits of a flying saucer that crashed.

The story of the crash was in the paper.

Here is the headline from the front page
of the paper.

Roswell Daily News

Air Force finds Flying Saucer on farm in Roswell

What a story! But was it true?

headline *The words at the top of a newspaper story*

The full story

2 July 1947

It was a dark wet night.

Something crashed.

What was it?

3 July 1947

A farmer called Mac found some bits from the crash.

He took them to the police.

Something crashed here. I'd better tell the police.

Come in!

COUNTY SHERIFF

'Something crashed on my land last night,'
said Mac. 'Here are some pieces from the crash.'

They were silver and bright. But they were
not metal.

What were they?

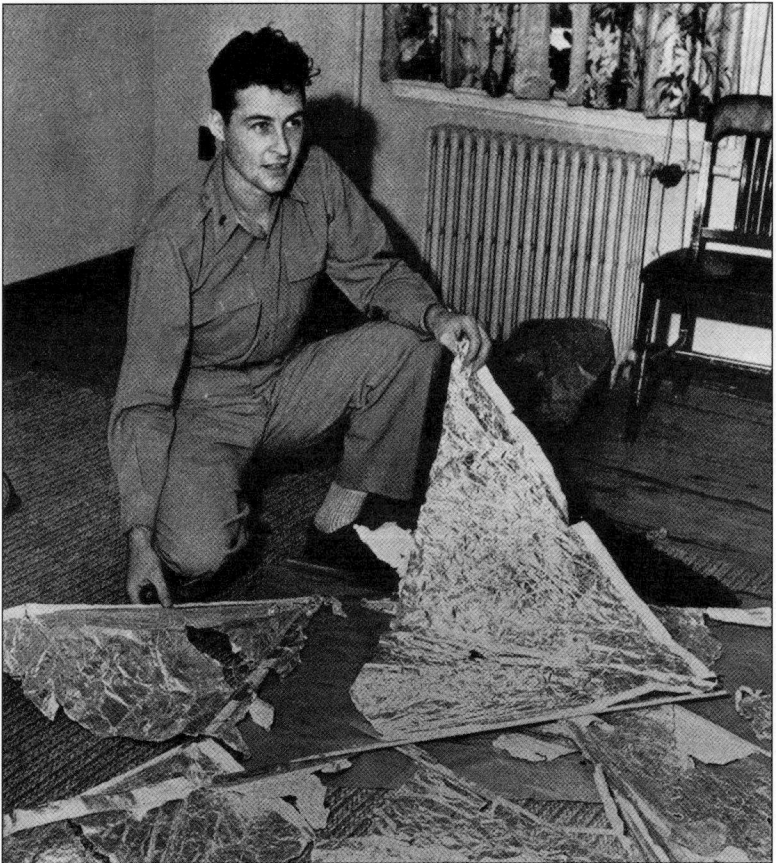

A man showing pieces from the crash

'I will call the Air Force,' said the policeman.
'Maybe they have lost a plane.'

He called the Air Force at Roswell.

Come and check it out.

OK. We're on our way.

ROSWELL ARMY AIR FORCE BASE

4 July 1947

Some Air Force men came to look at the crash.

'Don't talk about this,' they told Mac. 'It's top secret.'

They took the pieces away.

They put them on a plane.

They sent them to Washington DC.

Washington DC is the capital city of the USA.

capital city   *The most important city in a country*

8 July 1947 midday

A newspaper reporter wanted to know what had crashed.

He asked the Air Force.

They said it was a flying saucer.

So the story was put in the Roswell paper.

8 July 1947 2.00 p.m.

But two hours later a man in Washington told a different story.

'It wasn't a flying saucer that crashed. It was a weather balloon.'

Which story was true?

It wasn't a UFO after all. It was a weather balloon.

weather balloon   *A balloon that is used to find out facts about the weather*

Aliens from another world...?

Some people think the man from Washington was lying.

They say it was a cover-up.

It was really a UFO.

They believe there were aliens in the UFO.

There were several small bodies in the UFO.

They were aliens from another world.

They had big heads and large eyes.

aliens *Beings from another world*

...Or a weather balloon?

Other people think the UFO was just part of a weather balloon.

They say it was an Air Force balloon, made from a secret new material.

It was just a weather balloon.

The men at Roswell did not know about the weather balloon, because it was top secret.

That's why they said it was a UFO.

What do you think?

A weather balloon

Thirty-eight years later

New York, USA – 1995

A man said he had found an old film.

It showed two men cutting up a body.

'That's an alien,' the man said. 'It was in the Roswell UFO. You can buy the film from me and put it on TV.'

I want a lot of money for this film.

It is an old film, and it is in black and white.
It is not very clear.

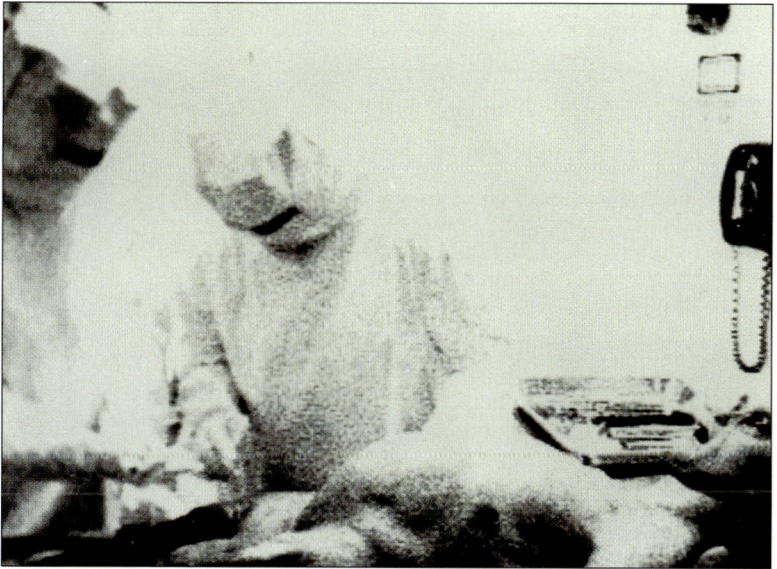

A picture from the film

UK – 1995

The film was on TV.

Some people think the body really was an alien's.

They believe a UFO crashed in 1947 with aliens in it.

They say the 'balloon' story was a cover-up.

Look. They're cutting up an alien.

These people believe the Roswell UFO was not the only one!

They say that lots of UFOs have crashed.

It is all a great big cover-up.

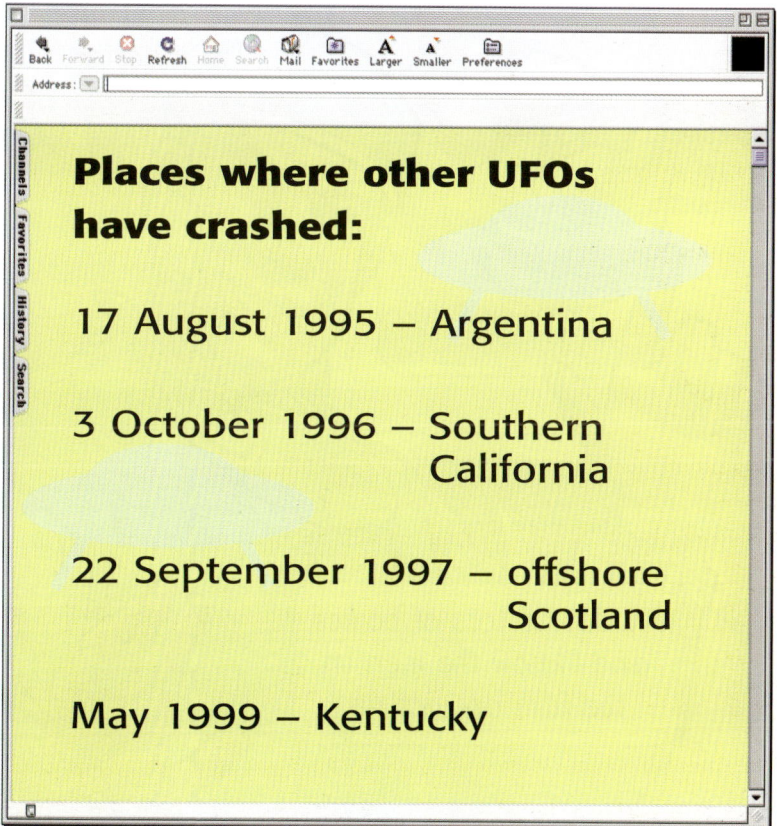

Places where other UFOs have crashed:

17 August 1995 – Argentina

3 October 1996 – Southern California

22 September 1997 – offshore Scotland

May 1999 – Kentucky

You can see a list on the Internet.

A true story?

Were they acting?

Lots of other people think the film is not true.

They say the people in the film were acting.

Wait a minute! I'm a doctor.

I've cut up lots of bodies, and I know the men in the film are acting.

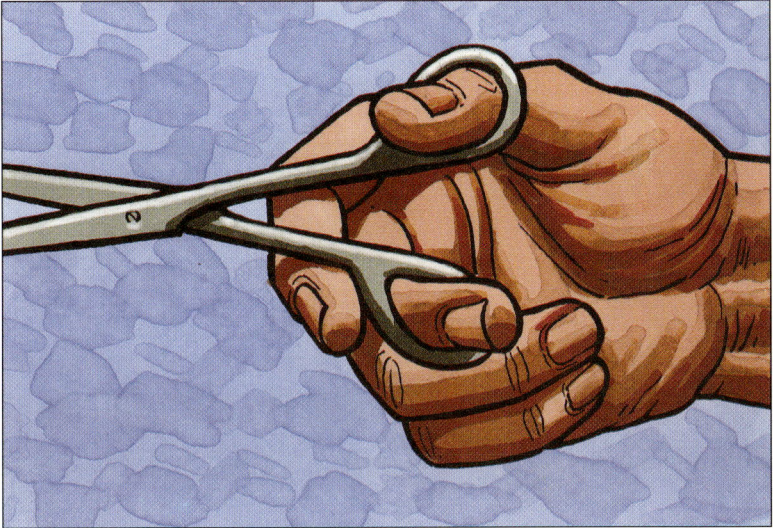

This is what a doctor really does.

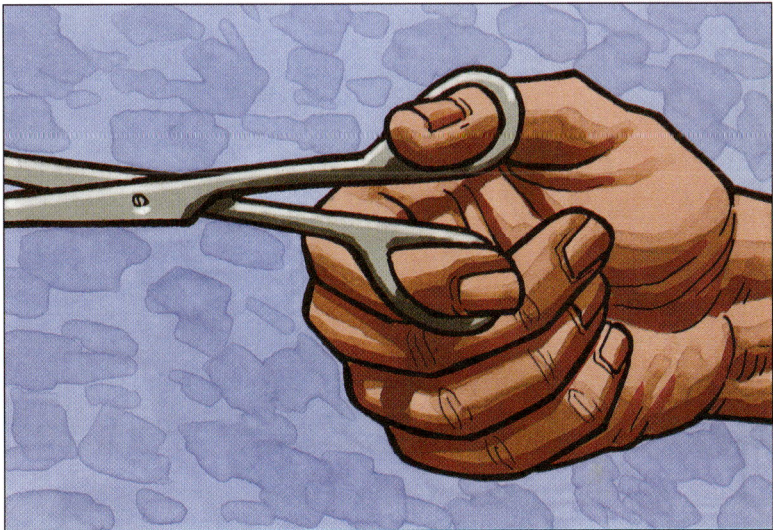

The men in the film do this.

Is it a dummy?

They say the body in the film is a dummy.

> I work in films.
> That body isn't an alien.
> It's a dummy.
> It isn't even a very good dummy!
> I've made lots of dummies, and I know.

dummy   *A figure that is made to look like another object or person*

How to make an alien

It is easy to make a dummy like the one in the film.

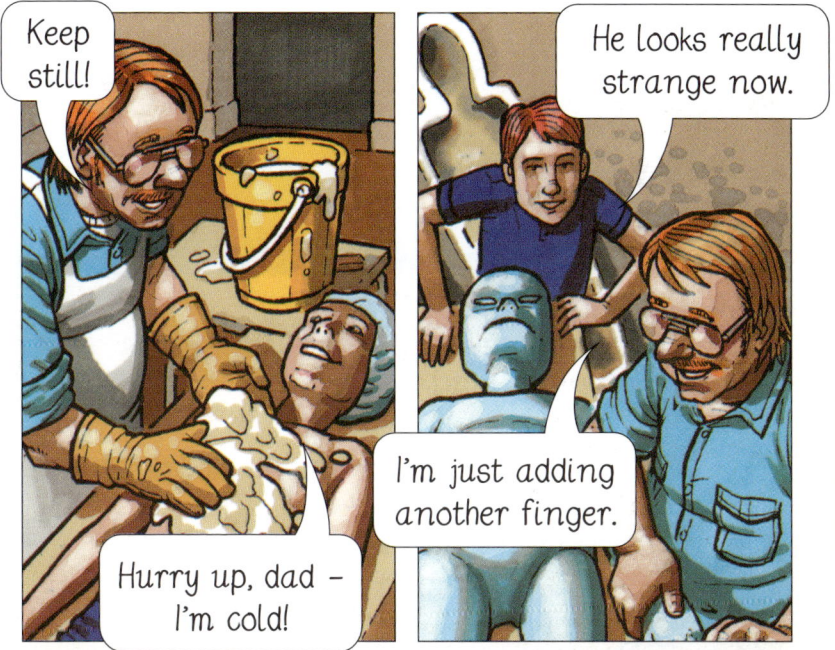

Keep still!

Hurry up, dad – I'm cold!

He looks really strange now.

I'm just adding another finger.

It looks just like the alien in the film.

Can you see how easy it is now?

What do you think?

That film is sometimes shown again on TV.

Perhaps you have seen it.

Was the body an alien?

Or was it a dummy?

BBC 1

8.00 **Alien or dummy?**
This old black-and-white film shows two men cutting up a body.
But is it an alien or a dummy?
'An alien,' says the man who found the film. 'It was in the UFO that crashed in Roswell in 1947.'
Make up your mind tonight!

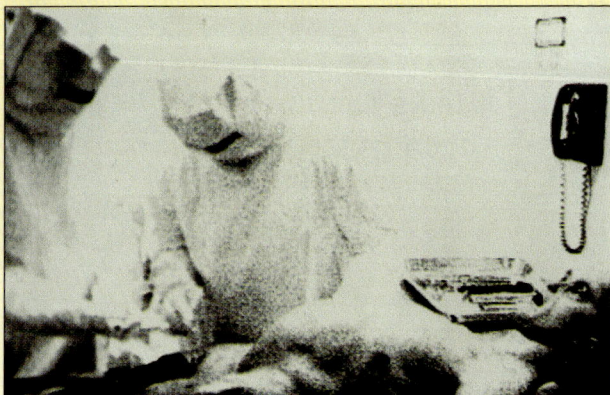

Who is right?
What do you think?

It was an alien!

It was a dummy!

Planet Earth

This is the Solar System.

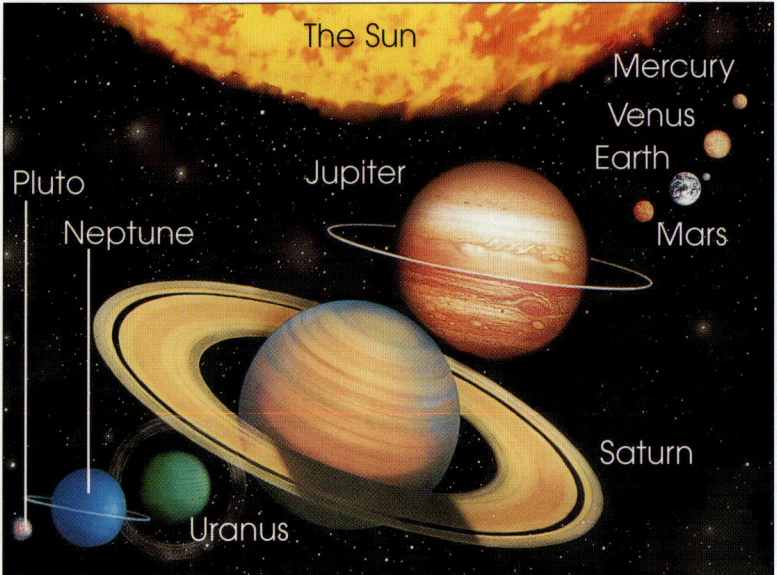

Solar means 'of the Sun.'

Nine planets go round the Sun.

We say that the planets 'orbit' the Sun.

planet   *A large round object in space which goes round the Sun or a star*

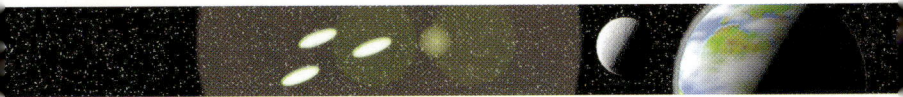

Our planet is called the Earth.

The Earth is the third planet from the Sun.

People used to think the Sun went round the Earth.

Third rock from the Sun –
that's the Earth!

Seeing stars

Our Sun is a star.

It is just one of billions of stars in the sky.

Long ago, people gave names to the stars.

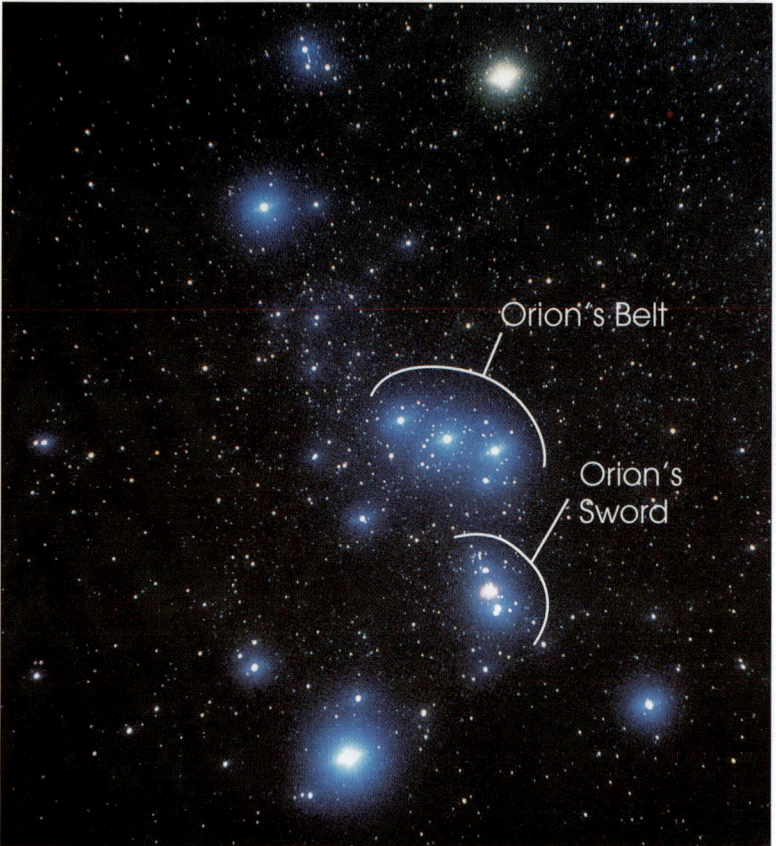

Orion's Belt

Orion's Sword

This group of stars is called Orion the Hunter.

billion *A very big number (a thousand million – 1,000,000,000)*

A telescope makes stars and planets look nearer and bigger.

The telescopes below were made by a man called Galileo in 1609.

Galileo saw spots on the Sun.

He saw Jupiter's moons.

Galileo and his telescopes

Big telescopes

Today we have very strong telescopes.

Some big telescopes can spot a firefly – or a UFO – 10,000 kilometres away.

Telescopes at Kitt Peak in Arizona

A firefly

This big telescope is in space.

It orbits the Earth and sends back pictures by radio.

It has found stars with planets orbiting them.

Maybe there is life on these planets.

The Hubble Space Telescope

Light years away

But those planets are many light years away.

A light year is the distance light travels in a year.

Light travels at 300,000 kilometres per second.

So light travels 9.5 million million kilometres per year.

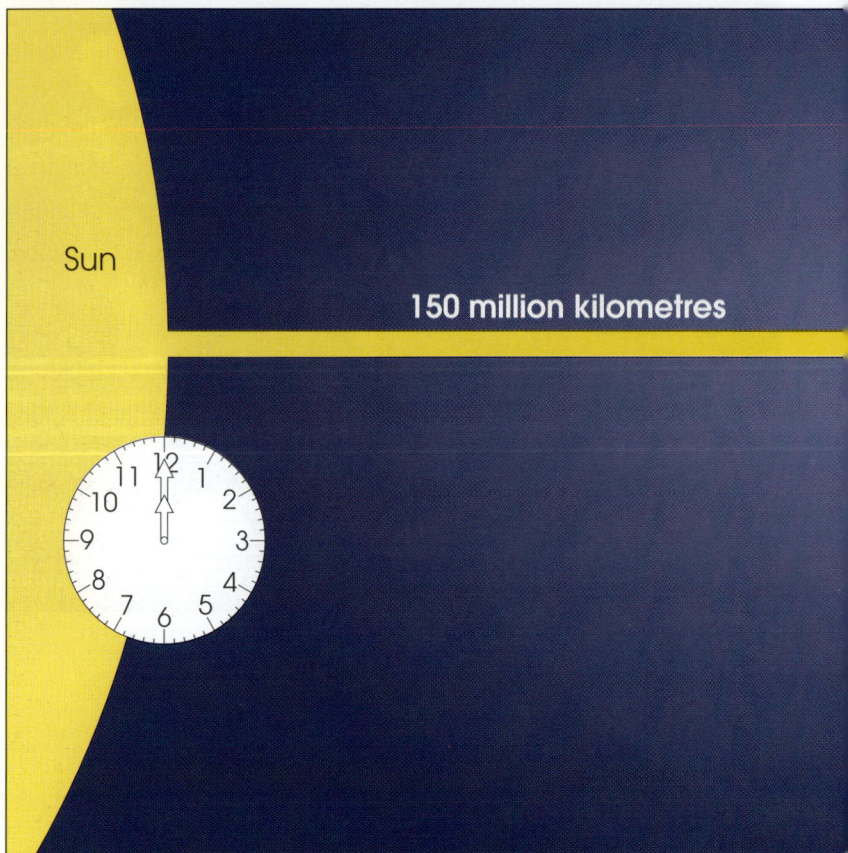

Sun

150 million kilometres

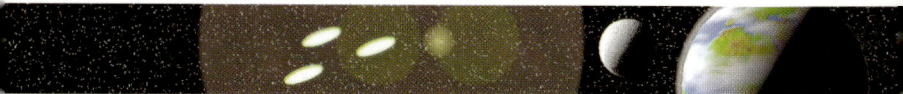

The Sun is 150 million kilometres from Earth.

The Sun's light takes 8 minutes to reach Earth.

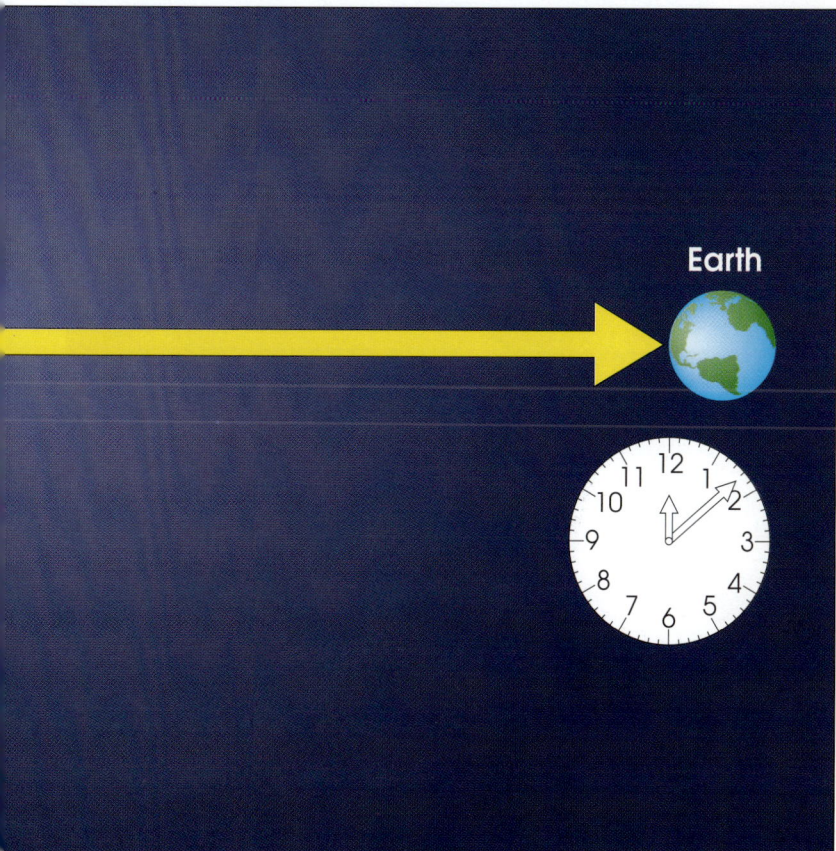

Looking for life

Are there aliens who are looking for us?
We don't know. But we are looking for them.

This spaceship travels far out into space.
It can send messages back to Earth.

A spaceship built to send messages back to Earth

This spaceship is called Voyager.

It carries facts about Earth.

It would help anyone who is out there to find us.

Voyager

Words to remember

aliens	Beings from another world
BC	BC stands for 'Before Christ'. It is used to measure time before the Year 0.
billion	A very big number (a thousand million – 1,000,000,000)
capital city	The most important city in a country
dummy	A figure that is made to look like another object or person
flying saucer	A flying object shaped like a saucer
headline	The words at the top of a newspaper story
light year	The distance light travels in a year
orbit	This means 'to go round'
planet	A large round object in space which goes round the Sun or a star
satellite	An object sent into space that goes around the Earth
shooting star	A piece of rock or metal that burns brightly when it comes close to the Earth
solar	This means 'of the Sun'
telescope	This is used to make objects that are far away look nearer and bigger
UFO	UFO stands for 'Unidentified Flying Object'. It is something that has been seen flying in the sky, but no one can say what it is.
weather balloon	A balloon that is used to find out facts about the weather